JACKIE ROBINSON

JACKIE ROBINSON

Richard Scott

GROLIER INCORPORATED
Danbury, Connecticut

Editor-in-Chief Nancy Toff

Executive Editor Remmel T. Nunn

Managing Editor Karyn Gullen Browne

Copy Chief Perry Scott King

Art Director Giannella Garrett

Picture Editor Elizabeth Terhune

Staff for JACKIE ROBINSON

Senior Editor Richard Rennert

Senior Designer Laurie Jewell

Copy Editors Sean Dolan, Gillian Bucky

Picture Research Judy Posner, Elie Porter

Production Coordinator Alma Rodriguez

Cover Illustration Alan J. Nahigian

Published for Grolier by Chelsea House

ISBN 0-7172 8556-1

CONTENTS

ON
ACHIEVEMENT

Coretta Scott King

BEFORE YOU BEGIN this book, I hope you will ask yourself what the word excellence means to you. I think that it's a question we should all ask, and keep asking as we grow older and change. Because the truest answer to it should never change. When you think of excellence, perhaps you think of success at work; or of becoming wealthy; or meeting the right person, getting married, and having a good family life.

Those important goals are worth striving for, but there is a better way to look at excellence. As Martin Luther King, Jr., said in one of his last sermons, "I want you to be first in love. I want you to be first in moral excellence. I want you to be first in generosity. If you want to be important, wonderful. If you want to be great, wonderful. But recognize that he who is greatest among you shall be your servant."

My husband, Martin Luther King, Jr., knew that the true meaning of achievement is service. When I met him, in 1952, he was already ordained as a Baptist preacher and was working towards a doctoral degree at Boston University. I was studying at the New England Conservatory and dreamed of accomplishments in music. We married a year later, and after I graduated the following year we moved to Montgomery, Alabama. We didn't know it then, but our notions of achievement were about to undergo a dramatic change.

You may have read or heard about what happened next. What began with the boycott of a local bus line grew into a national movement, and by the time he was assassinated in 1968 my husband had fashioned a black movement powerful enough to shatter forever the practice of racial segregation. What you may not have read about is where he got his method for resisting injustice without compromising his religious beliefs.

He got the strategy of nonviolence from a man of a different race, who lived in a distant country, and even practiced a different religion. The man was Mahatma Gandhi, the great leader of India, who devoted his life to serving humanity in the spirit of love and nonviolence. It was in these principles that Martin discovered his method for social reform. More than anything else, those two principles were the key to his achievements.

This book is about black Americans who served society through the excellence of their achievements. It forms a part of the rich history of black men and women in America—a history of stunning accomplishments in every field of human endeavor, from literature and art to science, industry, education, diplomacy, athletics, jurisprudence, even polar exploration.

Not all of the people in this history had the same ideals, but I think you will find something that all of them have in common. Like Martin Luther King, Jr., they all decided to become "drum majors" and serve humanity. In that principle—whether it was expressed in books, inventions, or song—they found something outside themselves to use as a goal and a guide. Something that showed them a way to serve others, instead of living only for themselves.

Reading the stories of these courageous men and women not only helps us discover the principles that we will use to guide our own lives, but it teaches us about our black heritage and about America itself. It is crucial for us to know the heroes and heroines of our history and to realize that the price we paid in our struggle for equality in America was dear. But we must also understand that we have gotten as far as we have partly because America's democratic system and ideals made it possible.

We still are struggling with racism and prejudice. But the great men and women in this series are a tribute to the spirit of our democratic ideals and the system in which they have flourished. And that makes their stories special, and worth knowing. ❧

JACKIE
ROBINSON

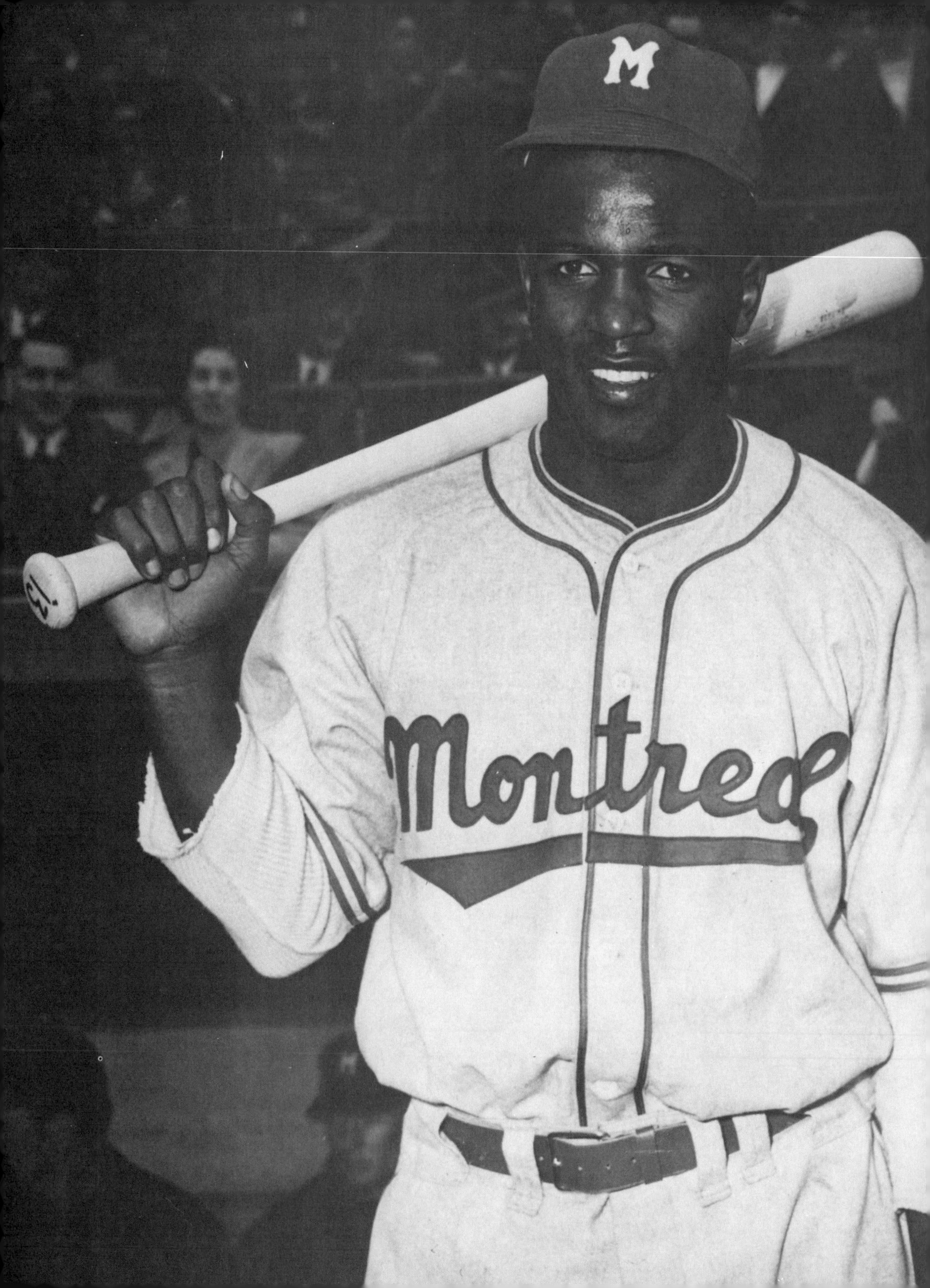
M
Montreal

1

THE EXPERIMENT BEGINS

O PENING DAY of a new baseball season brings a special kind of joy to baseball fans. For the beginning of a brand-new season marks a time of renewal and optimism as the pleasures of this summer game resurface after a long winter's wait. Favorite players and favorite teams are again given the opportunity to perform and excel, with routine plays and predictable outcomes once more giving way to the excitement of the unexpected.

For baseball fans in 1946, the start of the major league season held even more excitement and anticipation than usual. From 1940 on, many of the best ballplayers in America—including such stars as Joe DiMaggio of the New York Yankees, Ted Williams of the Boston Red Sox, and Stan Musial of the St. Louis Cardinals—had served in the armed forces. This mobilization continued through the mid-1940s, until more than half of the players who had been performing at the major league level in the early 1940s were instead fighting for their country in World War II. Their replacements on the ballfield were generally either overage or underage for military service and did not have as much experience and talent. It became quite obvious to almost any-

Robinson sharpened his baseball skills in the minor leagues with the Montreal Royals before he joined the Brooklyn Dodgers.

Few players in baseball history have been as skilled or as popular as Joe DiMaggio, the graceful center fielder for the New York Yankees.

one who attended a ball game during the war years that the presence of these substitute players lowered the overall quality of the game.

When the war was over and the top players returned to the playing fields in 1946, they were welcomed back by an unprecedented number of fans. Total attendance for the 16 major league teams nearly doubled from the previous years. However, it was not only a desire to see these returning players perform again that prompted the American public to go to ball games in such large numbers. In 1946 Americans found that they had more money than in the past to spend on entertainment. The war effort had helped the nation's economy, creating new industries and more jobs for a changing society just emerging from the throes of a great economic depression.

The war also prepared Americans for changes in society that were still to come. The United States had entered the war largely to help its allies fight the Nazis, the ruling party in Germany, who had been pursuing a course of racial prejudice and persecution on a worldwide scale. Being cast in the role of the great liberator reaffirmed America's vision of itself as a defender of democracy and human rights.

So it was that the events of the war left the American people more aware than ever before that their country had a responsibility to fight prejudice and persecution. Yet this awareness did not put a stop to racial discrimination in America—certainly not in the game of baseball. As the 1946 major league season began, blacks were not invited to join the ranks of returning major league ballplayers. In fact, most black Americans—many of whom had fought for their country during World War II—were still treated by their countrymen as second-class citizens once the war was over.

If blacks wanted to play professional ball in 1946, they had to do so in the segregated Negro Leagues, which had been in existence since 1920. A city councilman in New York summed up the senselessness of such segregation practices by distributing a flyer, depicting a dead black soldier and a black baseball player, with a caption that read: "Good enough to die for his country, but not good enough for organized baseball." A similar sense of outrage caused a number of other people to believe that perhaps the time was right for them, too, to see whether they could begin to put an end to such discriminatory policies.

An extremely shrewd man named Branch Rickey planned on doing just that. By the time he was

Women laborers, such as the ones shown here taking a break from building B-24 bombers, contributed mightily to the success of the U.S. effort during World War II.

The Philadelphia Stars, like most Negro baseball teams, started out playing whenever and wherever possible. They joined an organized league in the early 1930s, as the Negro Leagues became increasingly successful.

made president of the Brooklyn Dodgers in 1943, he had already established a reputation as one of the top executives in baseball history. Rickey has been credited with developing baseball's farm system, an organization that consists of major league teams controlling minor league franchises, with the minors refining the talents of young ballplayers for the parent club. This system helped to make the St. Louis Cardinals, for whom Rickey worked before he joined the Dodgers, a perennial top team in the National League for over 20 years.

Rickey's ambition to build a winning team in Brooklyn coincided perfectly with his desire to see blacks cross baseball's color line—a dream that Rickey had been hoping to make come true ever since he first saw how deeply racial discrimination could affect someone. When Rickey coached baseball at Ohio Wesleyan University in 1904, a black first baseman named Charlie Thomas was one of the best players on the team. On a road trip to play against Notre Dame, Thomas was refused a room at a hotel because he was black. Rickey talked the hotel manager into putting a cot for Thomas in Rickey's own room, as the hotel usually did for a black servant of a guest. Later that night, Rickey saw Thomas weep while rubbing his hands as though he were trying to rub off the color of his skin. "Black skin! Black skin!" Thomas kept saying. "If I could only make them white."

Witnessing Thomas's anguish that night had a powerful effect on Rickey. "That scene haunted me for many years," he said later, "and I vowed that I would always do whatever I could to see that other Americans did not have to face the bitter humiliation that was heaped upon Charles Thomas."

This promise was remembered by Rickey over the next 40 years as he waited for the right time for baseball's unwritten segregation laws to be challenged. When he started his search for black ballplayers with enough talent to play in the major

The Pittsburgh Crawfords, a star-studded team in the Negro Leagues, were led by catcher Josh Gibson (center).

Satchel Paige was one of the top pitchers in the Negro Leagues. He finally realized his lifelong dream of pitching in the major leagues in 1948, when he was signed by the Cleveland Indians.

leagues, he had to proceed with caution. Rickey knew that if word of his plan to integrate baseball leaked out, there would be a movement by those who were against integration to stop him, and his plan might ultimately fail. So Rickey developed a scheme to hide his real intentions: for two years he sent his talent scouts to Puerto Rico, Cuba, and all over America, telling them that they were looking for black players to make up a new team, which would be called either the Brown Dodgers or the Brown Bombers and would play in Brooklyn whenever the other Dodgers club was playing elsewhere. The scouts told Rickey about both the physical and the mental makeup of the candidates with the best chances of competing successfully in the major leagues. These players included such veteran stars of the Negro Leagues as Satchel Paige and Josh Gibson, as well as younger men such as Roy Campanella of the Baltimore Elite Giants and Don Newcombe of the Newark Eagles.

Rickey was not only looking for someone who would be a great success on the field, but for someone who would perform just as admirably away from the ballpark. The first black man to play in the major leagues had to be strong enough to withstand the abuse and the pressures that would most certainly come his way. He could let nothing shake his self-confidence or his self-esteem, for to do so would surely affect his ability to concentrate on the game—and then the entire experiment of having a black play major league ball would fail. But if he were to succeed—then no one could question a black man's right to play in the major leagues.

During the summer of 1945 Rickey determined that the one man who fit this description better than anyone else was Jackie Robinson, a 26-year-old shortstop for the Kansas City Monarchs. Three scouts had all agreed that this former All-American football player was an outstanding athlete, which prompted Rickey to travel to California, where Robinson had grown up, to check into his background. Rickey learned that Robinson, who had a college education and had been an army officer during the war, was very disciplined, yet also very aggressive. He seemed to have all of the character traits that would be necessary for handling all of the attention he would receive.

Robinson first met with Rickey on August 28, 1945, in Rickey's office in New York. Robinson had been asked to come there from Kansas City by a Dodger scout, who had relayed the usual fictional story that Rickey was looking for players for the Brown Bombers. Only after Robinson entered Rickey's office was he told the real reason for his visit. Rickey talked with Robinson for three hours, often speaking emotionally about the difficulties that the

Robinson (kneeling, first from left) played on a black all-star team that toured Venezuela just before he joined the Montreal Royals in 1946. Among his all-star teammates was Roy Campanella (standing, second from left).

first black ballplayer in the majors would encounter. Rickey repeatedly described to Robinson what his responsibilities would be if he were to join the Dodgers.

Robinson finally asked, "Mr. Rickey, do you want a ballplayer who's afraid to fight back?"

"I want a player with guts enough not to fight back," Rickey told him. The test for Robinson would be for him to shrug off any ugly comments and threats he might hear.

As Robinson sat in Rickey's office, he realized he would have to control his urge to fight. Instead of giving in to his anger, he would have to act

Branch Rickey began his brief playing career in 1905 with the St. Louis Browns. He later scouted for and managed the club before joining the St. Louis Cardinals and then the Brooklyn Dodgers.

passively. This would be an especially difficult thing for him to do, for he had been in the habit of fighting back ever since he was eight years old and a little girl from his neighborhood had taunted him with racist remarks.

Robinson had always thought of himself as someone who would not back down from a fight of any kind. Yet that was what Rickey was asking him to consider doing now—for the sake of an even greater fight. It took him almost five full minutes to think over Rickey's proposal before he broke the silence. "If you want to take this gamble, I will promise you there will be no incident," Robinson said. ❧

Baseball history is made: Robinson signs a contract to play with the Montreal Royals on October 23, 1945.

2

A
DETERMINATION
TO WIN

J ACK ROOSEVELT ROBINSON was born on January 31, 1919, the grandson of a slave and the youngest of five children of Mallie and Jerry Robinson. He was only six months old when his father, who was a sharecropper barely earning a living on a plantation near Cairo, Georgia, left the family to seek his fortunes elsewhere. Determined to give her children a chance at a better life, Jackie's mother moved them to Pasadena, California, a mostly white suburb near Los Angeles. She bought a house on Pepper Street with the aid of a welfare agency, only to have her white neighbors petition to have her family relocated. Although this effort failed, she and her children were often harassed by nearby residents and had to turn to one another for strength and comfort.

Robinson's mother taught her children not to be bullied by such treatment. "I remember, even as a small boy, having a lot of pride in my mother," Jackie later recalled. "I thought she must have had some kind of magic to be able to do all the things she did, to work so hard and never complain and to make us all feel happy. We had our family squabbles and spats, but we were a well-knit unit."

While Mallie Robinson worked by doing household chores for other families, her children—Edgar, Frank, Mack, and Willa Mae, as well as Jackie—

While Robinson was a student at UCLA, he won the national collegiate championship in the long jump.

Track-and-field star Jesse Owens on his way to winning one of four gold medals in the 1936 Olympic Games held in Berlin.

went to school and played sports in their free time. One of Jackie's older brothers, Mack, eventually became a world-class sprinter. In 1936 he went to Berlin and competed in the 200-meter dash in the Olympics, finishing second in the event only to Jesse Owens, one of America's greatest black track stars, who went on to win an unprecedented four gold medals during those Olympic Games.

Along with going to school and playing sports, Jackie spent his time while growing up with a gang of local boys who played schoolboy pranks on their neighbors. They stole food from grocery stands, threw clumps of dirt at passing cars, and swiped golf balls from the local golf course and then sold the balls back to their owners. Hardly a week went by without Jackie and his friends having to report to a youth officer at the neighborhood police station.

Jackie was well on his way to becoming a juvenile delinquent by the time he was a teenager. However, he was fortunate enough to attract the attention of Carl Anderson, a mechanic who worked near the Pepper Street gang's hangout. Anderson told Jackie that if he continued to run around with the gang, his actions would one day come back to hurt his mother. All he was doing was following the crowd, which was an easy thing to do. The idea was to try to be different.

Anderson's words and the influence of Reverend Karl Downs helped Jackie to separate from the gang. The pastor at the Robinson family's church, Reverend Downs befriended Jackie and helped him through difficult times. The strength of their friendship eventually inspired Jackie to volunteer to teach Sunday school at a time when doing so was often difficult, as it meant rising early in the morning while feeling sore and bruised from a football game the day before.

Such devotion to his responsibilities helped Jackie at John Muir Technical High School, where he excelled as an athlete, earning letter awards in football, basketball, baseball, and track. Conflicting sports schedules and fierce competition could not stop him. Given constant encouragement by his brothers, he became aggressive and determined to win.

Other teams often singled him out. "They decided that I was the best man to beat," Jackie said. "I enjoyed having that kind of reputation, but I was also very much aware of the importance of being a team man, not jeopardizing my team's chances simply to get the spotlight."

Robinson earned All-American honors in football while attending UCLA.

In both of Robinson's seasons with the UCLA basketball team, he was the team's leading scorer.

Robinson hoped to be awarded an athletic scholarship to a major university during his last year in high school, but none was offered. He enrolled at Pasadena Junior College, where he led the basketball, football, and baseball teams to championships and also continued to pursue his interest in track and field. On a May morning in 1938 he began the best day of his junior college career. At a track meet in Pomona, California, he participated in the long jump, having received special permission to take his jumps early in the morning, before the meet officially began. His third and final jump was for 25 feet, 6½ inches—good enough to win the meet and set a new record. Robinson then journeyed to Glendale, California, where he played shortstop for his junior college team as they won the championship that afternoon. The day's performance capped a great two-year career at Pasadena and led many major universities to offer him a scholarship for his final two years of athletic eligibility.

Robinson chose the University of California at Los Angeles (UCLA), which was close to his home. Although he often felt out of place at such a wealthy and traditional school, he was right at home on its playing fields. Robinson became the school's first four-letter man, meaning that no one before him had made four varsity athletic teams. Robinson played basketball, football, and baseball and ran track at UCLA. He led the basketball conference in scoring for two years in a row, won the national championship in the long jump, was named as an All-American halfback, and traveled to Chicago and Hawaii to participate in all-star football games.

While Robinson was at UCLA he also won the affections of Rachel Isum. They first met in 1940, when he was a 21-year-old senior and she was a freshman nursing student. Robinson later admitted, "I was immediately attracted to Rachel's looks and charm, but as in many love stories, I didn't have the slightest idea I was meeting a young lady who would become the most important person in my life." Rachel and Jackie did not get married until the winter of 1946—shortly after he signed his first contract to play with the Dodgers—yet their constant support and devotion to one another following their first meeting were to prove invaluable during the difficult times that lay ahead.

In the spring of 1941 Robinson decided to leave UCLA even though he had not yet earned his

Six years after they first met, Robinson was married to Rachel Isum in Los Angeles, in 1946, by Jackie's friend Reverend Karl Downs.

Always seeking to distinguish himself, Robinson managed to become an officer—a second lieutenant—in the army by the time he was twenty-four years old.

degree. He was convinced "that no amount of education would help a black man get a job. I felt I was living in an academic and athletic dream world," he said. "It seemed very necessary for me to relieve some of my mother's financial burdens even though I knew it had always been her dream to have me finish college."

Robinson would have preferred to earn a living by playing sports on a professional level, but since he had little hope of doing so because he was black, he decided to remain in sports in another way: by becoming an athletic director for the National Youth Administration. He greatly enjoyed this job, which entailed working with disadvantaged children. In his spare time he played football with a semiprofessional team, which gave him some extra income for supporting his mother.

In 1942, one year after leaving school, Robinson was drafted by the army and sent to Fort Riley, Kansas, for basic training. He completed his training and applied for admission to Officer's Candidate School, which trained special soldiers to become officers. Although Robinson and some other black soldiers seemed to qualify for admission because they had attended college and passed all of the required exams, they were not allowed to enroll because they were black.

This was the first of several racial confrontations that Robinson would encounter while in the army. Characteristically, he did not sit still; he chose to fight back. Joe Louis, the black prizefighter who was then heavyweight champion of the world, was also stationed at Fort Riley. Robinson told him about the problem, and Louis used his influence to get Robinson and the other blacks admitted to the school. In January 1943 he became a second lieutenant.

Word of Robinson's prowess as an All-American athlete led to his being asked to play on the military

base's football team against college teams and other military teams. Robinson practiced with the team but then learned that the first game of the season was to be against the University of Missouri—a school that refused to play against a team with a black player. The army complied with Missouri's ultimatum and attempted to sidestep the issue with Robinson by giving him leave for the time at which the game was to be played. Robinson enjoyed the leave but recognized the army's evasion for what it was and left the squad, refusing to return even when a colonel threatened to order him to play. He would

Sergeant Joe Louis, the heavyweight champion of the world, offers some boxing tips to his fellow soldiers at Fort Riley, Kansas.

At one time in American history, racial segregation seemed to touch all aspects of daily life.

not play for a team that through its own actions condoned racial discrimination.

Robinson also sought to join the baseball team while he was at Fort Riley but encountered an even more direct snub. Pete Reiser, who later became Robinson's teammate on the Dodgers, was present when Robinson attempted to join the team:

One day a Negro lieutenant came out for the ball team. An officer told him he couldn't play. "You have to play with the colored team," the officer said. That was a joke. There was no colored team. The lieutenant didn't say anything. He stood there for a while watching us work out. Then he turned and walked away. I didn't know who he was then, but that was the first time I saw Jackie Robinson. I can still remember him walking away by himself.

Another incident occurred when Robinson was asked to look into the lack of seating for blacks at the army base's center. He called company headquarters to explain the problem, only to be told over the phone by a fellow officer, who had no idea the person he was talking to was black, "How would you like to have your wife sitting next to a nigger?" Robinson's rage over this comment eventually led to the problem being settled, but soon after this he was transferred to Fort Hood, Texas, and ran into even bigger problems.

One evening in July 1944 Robinson was returning to the base by bus, talking with a fellow lieutenant's wife, who happened to be white. The bus driver stopped the bus and told Robinson to sit in the back of the bus, where the seats were reserved for blacks. Robinson ignored the driver's commands, aware that Joe Louis and another black fighter, Ray Robinson, had recently refused to sit in the backs of buses; their refusals and the publicity that followed had caused the army to bar discriminatory seating on any of its vehicles. The driver stopped the bus for a second time, screaming that he could make plenty of trouble for Robinson if he did not move.

"I told him hotly that I couldn't care less about his causing me trouble," Robinson said. "I'd been in trouble all my life, but I knew what my rights were."

When the bus ride ended, the driver summoned the military police to take charge of the matter. Robinson went peacefully with them to talk to their captain, fully expecting the whole incident to be cleared up quickly. To his surprise, Robinson soon found himself facing a military court-martial for his disobedience.

Since Robinson had acted within his rights, he was found innocent. However, he was tagged as a troublemaker and was not permitted to fight overseas. He received an honorable discharge from the

While Robinson was stationed with the army in Fort Hood, Texas, the Deep South continued to be the bastion of racial segregation in America, and scenes like the one shown here continued to be commonplace.

Even after the army did away with some of its discriminatory practices in the mid-1940s, soldiers such as this one still had to face racial segregation when they returned to civilian life.

army in November 1944 and returned home prouder and more defiant than ever before. His experiences in the army had sharpened his determination to stand up for his rights. As Branch Rickey once observed, "If he had done the things people are criticizing him for as a white . . . he would have been praised to the skies as a fighter, a holler guy, a real competitor, a ballplayer's ballplayer. But because he's black his aggressiveness is offensive to some."

After leaving the army Robinson joined the Kansas City Monarchs, a team in one of the Negro

Leagues, as a shortstop. He earned $400 a month, a large amount in 1945. However, life in the Negro Leagues was not very easy.

Living conditions were deplorable. Teams traveled by bus over bumpy roads neglected during the war years. Many hotels and restaurants did not serve blacks, so the black players often had to sleep and eat on the bus.

Just as discouraging was the obscurity of the Negro Leagues. Talented black ballplayers often toiled for years without attaining the recognition and adulation they deserved. Josh Gibson, for example, who played until the late 1940s, may have hit more home runs than the legendary Babe Ruth (the Negro Leagues did not always keep records of their games, so this is uncertain), yet Gibson's name is relatively unknown among baseball fans. "In those days a white ballplayer could look forward to some streak of luck or some reward for hard work to carry him into prominence or even stardom. What had the black player to hope for?" Robinson wondered. "What was his future?"

For most, it was bleak. Robinson often thought, "If I left baseball, where could I go, what could I do to earn enough money to help my mother and to marry Rachel?" Yet his future turned out bright—thanks to Branch Rickey.

Persuaded by Rickey to leave the Kansas City Monarchs after playing with them for only one season, Robinson signed a contract to join the Montreal Royals, the Dodgers' top minor league club, in the spring of 1946. He was to receive a salary of $600 a month and a signing bonus of $3,500. Robinson kept the news of his signing a secret for almost two months—until Rickey and the Dodgers had taken care of other business matters and were ready to reveal the start of what was to be called "baseball's great experiment." Their revelation resulted in

By the time the search for the first black major leaguer began in the mid-1940s, Josh Gibson, known as "the black Babe Ruth," was nearing the end of his career.

either outrage or jubilation all across America. Everyone, it seemed, had an opinion about how integration would affect the game. Yet one simple fact remained: despite all of the talk about Jackie Robinson breaking the color barrier, he had not yet played a single game for the Dodger organization. He still had to earn his way onto the major league roster.

Spring training in 1946 was to provide the first clue as to whether Robinson would succeed with the "experiment." He reported in February to preseason camp in Florida, where strict segregation laws were still enforced, and immediately showed that he could

Branch Rickey's well-planned antidiscriminatory efforts earned him the nickname "Mahatma," after the visionary Indian leader Mohandas K. Gandhi.

handle the situation by saying, "I'm going there to play ball, not to live. . . . I'll be down there strictly as a ballplayer and will act accordingly." Still, he had to contend with the other ballplayers, coaches, and the manager.

Clay Hopper, the man whom Rickey had chosen to manage Robinson and the rest of the Montreal Royals, was a plantation owner from the Deep South. Hopper never showed any prejudice toward Robinson, although years later it was revealed that he had begged Rickey not to send Robinson to play on his team. "Please don't do this to me," Hopper had pleaded with Rickey. "I'm white and I've lived in Mississippi all of my life. If you do this, you're going to force me to move my family and home out of Mississippi." Fortunately for Robinson, Rickey ignored Hopper's cries, for Hopper, a smart baseball man, proved to be the perfect choice for preparing Robinson for the major league game.

In the spring of 1946 the Dodger organization divided its training camp into two separate groups. The Dodgers trained in one group while the Royals practiced in another. In early March they met for the first time in an exhibition game. Robinson did not play very well in the game or in any of the other spring training games. Bothered by a sore arm as well as some unpleasant experiences—racist regulations in the South did not allow him to play in some of the ballparks—he looked as though he would have a very difficult time in integrated big league baseball.

The Montreal Royals opened the 1946 International League season on April 18 against the hometown Jersey City Giants. The ballpark was not far from New York City and packed with nearly 30,000 fans. They had not only come to see the return of baseball after the war but to watch Jackie Robinson make his first minor league appearance.

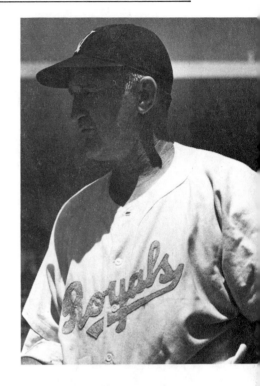

Clay Hopper drew on knowledge gained from years of baseball experience to manage Robinson and the Montreal Royals to the Little World Series title in 1946.

Clyde Sukeforth, the Dodger scout who contacted Robinson when he was still with the Kansas City Monarchs.

More than half a year had passed since he had signed to play for Montreal, and people had come from all over to see the momentous event.

Robinson was the second player to bat in the game, and he seemed very nervous as he approached the plate. He tried not to get distracted by the large crowd, which included his wife, Rachel; he tried to concentrate solely on the game. However, the tension of the moment made his hands "too moist to grip the bat," and all he could manage to hit was a routine ground ball to the shortstop. Robinson was easily out at first.

He came up to bat again in the third inning. Two runners were on base with no outs, so the Giants expected Robinson, a masterful bunter, to lay one down and move the runners over. Yet instead of trying to place a bunt, he took a full swing—and hit a three-run home run over the left-field fence. A huge smile appeared on his face as he circled the bases. It was just the first of many smiles that day.

After bunting for a base hit in the fifth inning, Robinson stole second base. Once there, he began to dance off the bag in a way that would unnerve opposing players for years to come. When the next Montreal batter hit a grounder to the third baseman, Robinson broke for third base as soon as the fielder started to throw the ball across the diamond and made it safely.

Taking a long lead from third, he prompted the pitcher to throw over to the bag in an attempt to hold him close to the base. Yet Robinson did not stay close. He started running toward home on the first pitch—only to stop when he was halfway down the line and race back to the bag. It grew obvious to the crowd—as it had to the Giants' pitcher—that Robinson was planning on stealing home, and everyone began to cheer, hoping that this rare and exciting play would take place. On the next pitch Robinson sprinted down the line again, causing the pitcher to illegally alter his pitching motion (balk) in an attempt to throw him out, and he was allowed by the umpires to proceed safely home. The huge crowd went wild, fully appreciating the combination of power and speed that the Royals' new second baseman was showing them.

In the seventh inning Robinson singled, stole another base, and scored another run. In the eighth he again bunted safely, crossed from first to third on an infield hit and again was balked home after his dashing act from third.

Robinson went four-for-five for the day as the Royals won, 14–1. He scored four runs, drove in three, and stole two bases, all the while exciting the crowd. "This would have been a big day for any man," *The New York Times* reported, "but under the

Robinson slides safely into third base in his first minor league game, on April 18, 1946, against the Jersey City Giants.

Robinson played shortstop for the Kansas City Monarchs in 1945 but was shifted to second base once he joined the Dodger organization.

special circumstances, it was a tremendous feat." In his first game Jackie Robinson had shown everyone that he could play baseball.

By the time the Royals reached Montreal, Robinson had hit safely in 10 of the team's first 12 games and scored 17 runs, helping the team dominate the rest of the International League. They often won games by large margins, and Robinson's play made him a beloved sports figure in Montreal. Children hounded him for autographs, while adults

poured into the ballpark to see him steal bases and score runs. As a Montreal sportswriter noted, "For Jackie Robinson and the city of Montreal, it was love at first sight."

Outside Canada, fans were much less kind. At a game in Baltimore, Maryland, they yelled racial slurs at him for nine straight innings. In Indianapolis, Indiana, he was pulled from a game because of a law prohibiting interracial athletics. In Syracuse, New York, an opposing player threw a black cat

Red Barber, the famous broadcaster for the Dodgers, helped spread the word of Robinson's exciting style of play via radio.

onto the field and hollered to Robinson that it was his cousin. The game was stopped by the umpire so that he could warn the Syracuse players about their behavior.

The worst incident happened during the Little World Series, a seven-game series that pitted the Royals, champions of the International League, against the Louisville Colonels, winners of the American Association title. Racial tension had been building in Louisville, Kentucky, before the series started, since the Colonels set quotas on how many black fans could attend home games.

Robinson fell into a deep hitting slump and played poorly during the three games in Louisville. He said, "I had been booed pretty soundly before, but nothing like this. A torrent of mass hatred burst from the stands with virtually every move I made." He managed only one hit in 11 at-bats as the Royals lost two of the first three games.

The Montreal fans heard about the abuse Robinson had suffered from the nearly all-white crowds in Louisville and were enraged. When the series returned to Canada, throngs of fans showed up to support Robinson in the remaining games. Each time a Louisville player stepped up to bat, the crowd released a deafening chorus of boos. "I didn't approve of this kind of retaliation," Robinson said, "but I felt a jubilant sense of gratitude for the way the Canadians expressed their feelings."

The fans' support helped Robinson to break his slump, and he in turn helped the Royals to battle back and win three straight games—and the championship. After the last win the crowd poured onto the field, chanting Robinson's name. They then hoisted the young ballplayer above their shoulders and paraded him around the field. Sam Martin, a Montreal sportswriter, described the day's scene as "probably the only day in history that a black man ran from a white mob with love instead of lynching on its mind."

Later in the clubhouse, Clay Hopper, the manager who had once asked Branch Rickey to keep Robinson off the team, told him, "You're a great ballplayer and a fine gentleman. It's been wonderful having you on the team." ❧

DODGERS
CLUB HOUSE

KEEP OUT

3

TURNING
THE
OTHER CHEEK

A S SPRING TRAINING approached in 1947, Branch Rickey planned Robinson's move from the Montreal Royals to the Brooklyn Dodgers with great care. Rickey knew the promotion would meet with opposition, so he devised a twofold plan to gain the support of his players and the fans. First, he decided to hold spring training for both the Montreal Royals and the Brooklyn Dodgers in Havana, Cuba, so as to avoid the segregation of the Deep South. Rickey hoped that once the Brooklyn players saw Robinson's talents on a daily basis, they would demand his promotion to the big league team. Next, Rickey invited three other black ballplayers—Roy Campanella, Don Newcombe, and Roy Partlow—to spring training. Rickey hoped that this move would help the Brooklyn ballplayers get acquainted with black athletes. In spite of these efforts, Rickey's plan did not work. The Dodgers refused to accept Robinson—some even signed a petition stating that they would not play baseball if Robinson were allowed on the team. Rickey was outraged and called the instigators of this action into his office, telling them that if they did not tear up the petition, they were off the team. The petition disappeared.

Rickey knew then not to expect support from the players, so he concocted a new plan. If the Brooklyn fans were to discover Robinson's talents,

Robinson's expert play on the field soon made him a welcome presence in the Dodgers' clubhouse.

When Dodger manager Leo Durocher (seated in center) returned from his 1947 suspension from baseball, he said of Robinson, "He didn't just come to play, he came to beat you."

they would demand that he play for the Dodgers. He told Robinson before he was to play with the Royals in a series of exhibition games against the Dodgers, "I want you to be a whirling demon against the Dodgers. I want you to concentrate, to hit the ball, to get on base *by any means possible*. . . . Not only will you impress the Dodger players, but the stories that the newspapermen send back to the Brooklyn and New York newspapers will help create demand on the part of the fans that you be brought up to the majors."

Robinson responded by playing spectacularly. His spring-training performance was clearly the best by any player of either club, but prejudice remained difficult to overcome. Few Brooklyn fans and players urged Rickey to put Robinson on the Dodgers' major league roster.

In a last ditch effort to win hometown support, Rickey asked Dodger manager Leo Durocher to tell sportswriters that Robinson's talent could help the Dodgers win the pennant. Before Durocher could make the statement, he was suspended from baseball for socializing with a known gambler. The incident resulted in bad publicity for the Dodgers, yet Rickey saw it as an opportunity to make the move he had been contemplating for some time. He erased the Durocher story from the sports pages with an even larger story: he promoted Robinson to the major leagues.

Robinson batted for the first time in the major leagues on April 15, 1947. He swung hard, lashed the ball sharply to the shortstop, and was thrown out by a half-step at first base. He made three more outs that first day and continued to play poorly through the first week of the season. Many fans questioned his talents, and even Robinson began to wonder whether he should be playing for the Dodgers.

Ben Chapman, the manager of the Philadelphia Phillies, adopts a friendly pose with Robinson shortly after Chapman led his team in a vicious verbal assault on the Dodger rookie.

To add to his problems, Robinson soon faced one of the worst moments in his baseball career. It occurred during a three-game series with the Philadelphia Phillies at Ebbets Field in Brooklyn. During his first trip to home plate, Robinson was bombarded by racial taunts and insults. "I could scarcely believe my ears," he said later. "Almost as if it had been synchronized by some master conductor, hate poured forth from the Phillies dugout."

There *was* a master conductor. The Philadelphia Phillies' manager, Ben Chapman, directed the attack from deep inside the dugout. Born in Alabama,

The Dodgers' starting infield in 1947 featured (from left to right) Spider Jorgensen, Pee Wee Reese, Eddie Stanky, and Jackie Robinson.

where segregation was still popular, Chapman admittedly did not like blacks. "At no time in my life have I heard racial venom and dugout abuse to match the abuse that Ben sprayed on Robinson that night," said one of Rickey's aides.

Robinson felt helpless against such assaults, since a direct response would endanger the great experiment. He wondered, "What did the Phillies want from me? What, indeed, did Mr. Rickey expect from me? I was, after all, a human being. What was I doing there turning the other cheek as though I weren't a man?" In his mind he played out a reply:

"I could throw down my bat, stride over to that Phillies dugout, grab one of [them] . . . and smash his teeth in with my despised black fist." Instead, he breathed deeply and resumed playing. The moment was the closest, Robinson said, that he came to using physical violence on the ball field. Although he remained silent, his teammates yelled back loudly at the Phillies on Robinson's behalf.

"Listen, you yellow-bellied cowards," screamed a Dodger player towards the Phillies' dugout, "why don't you yell at somebody who can answer back?"

"If you guys played as well as you talked, you'd win some games!" hollered another Dodger teammate.

After the game the Dodgers told some sports-writers about the Phillies' terrible conduct. Major newspapers ran editorials condemning Phillies man-

Robinson covers first base as Phil Rizzuto races for the bag during an exhibition game with the New York Yankees just before the start of the 1947 season.

ager Ben Chapman, while Robinson's control and sportsmanship won great respect. The New York *Daily Mirror* reported, "Jackie, with admirable restraint, ignored the guttersnipe language coming from the Phillies' dugout, thus stamping himself as the only gentleman among those involved in the incident."

Such animosity was not confined to that single incident. Richie Ashburn, a Phillies player who joined the club the following year, said, "When Jackie played second base, almost every Phillies runner went after him. We thought it was the thing to do. I nailed him on a double play one day and learned a valuable lesson. I cut him on his leg with my spikes. As he was lying there on the ground bleeding, I remembered thinking that his blood was the same color as mine. I vowed I would never intentionally try to injure another ballplayer."

The episode with Philadelphia served to unite the Dodgers. The players began to accept Robinson as a teammate and as a friend. What Branch Rickey had failed to accomplish with his intricate plans, the Philadelphia Phillies achieved with contemptible behavior. In one of baseball's darkest moments, Jackie Robinson had become a welcome member of the Brooklyn Dodgers.

Pee Wee Reese, the Dodgers' shortstop, demonstrated the extent of Robinson's acceptance during a game in Boston against the Braves. Reese was destined to be inducted into baseball's Hall of Fame, and Robinson greatly admired his talents. But Reese was born in the Deep South, where racial prejudice was strong, and the two ballplayers did not talk much during the first few weeks of the season.

All that changed, however, once the Boston fans tried to intimidate Robinson with insults. When Robinson stood silent, the hecklers soon turned their attention to Reese, asking him how a Southern gentleman could play baseball with a black.

National League President Ford Frick offered his full support to Robinson when it was discovered that the other teams were seeking to keep major league baseball all white.

Robinson (below arrow) amidst a group of black fans celebrating the Dodgers' pennant-clinching victory over Philadelphia.

Reese did not respond verbally. Instead, he left his position and walked over to Robinson. The two exchanged friendly words. Then Reese put one of his arms around Robinson's shoulders in a brotherly gesture intended to show support for Robinson. This not only quieted the crowd but led to Reese and Robinson becoming close friends.

However, not all ballplayers accepted Robinson's presence. In May 1947 the St. Louis Cardinals secretly conspired to hold a protest strike, voting to boycott a game with the Brooklyn Dodgers. They hoped other teams would follow suit and thereby force Robinson from the major leagues.

A newspaper discovered the plot and printed the story. Ford Frick, the National League president, immediately defended Robinson's right to play major league baseball. "If you do this you will be suspended from the league," Frick told the St. Louis ballplayers. "The National League will go down the line with Robinson whatever the consequences." It was the league's strongest statement in defense of Robinson's right to play baseball.

Supported by his teammates and league officials, Robinson gained confidence and soon began playing outstanding baseball. He ripped line drives and made spectacular defensive plays. He ran the bases like few men had done before. Dodger fans marveled at such athletic ability and began to appreciate his value as a ballplayer. Black fans in particular loved Jackie Robinson. To them, he symbolized a new future. Robinson had cracked the white man's world. Now other blacks could follow. Robinson said, "In a very real sense, black people helped make the experiment succeed. Many who came to the ballpark had not been baseball fans before I began to play in the big leagues. Suppressed and repressed for so many years, they needed a victorious black man as a symbol. It would help them believe in themselves."

Blacks turned out in droves to watch Jackie Robinson play, coming to Brooklyn by subway from

Robinson slides into second base under New York Yankees short-stop Phil Rizzuto during the 1947 World Series—the first of Robinson's six appearances in the fall classic.

New York City, by bus from Philadelphia, by train from the South. Blacks who had never before followed baseball became devoted Brooklyn Dodger fans. The games took on a festive atmosphere. In the grandstands black spectators openly celebrated their pride in Robinson's accomplishments.

Robinson and Rickey worried about the enthusiastic show of support. They feared that the tremendous response might eventually cause disturbances in the grandstands. Robinson admitted, "The breakthrough created as much danger as it did hope. It was one thing for me out there on the playing field to be able to keep my cool in the face of insults. But it was another for all those black people sitting in the stands to keep from overreacting when they sensed a racial slur or an unjust decision. They could have blown the whole bit to hell by acting belligerently and touching off a race riot. That would have been all the bigots needed to set back the cause of progress of black men in sports another hundred years." Rickey consequently began programs to avoid racial problems. He met with black community leaders and asked them to control their actions at the ballpark.

The message was passed by word of mouth. Brooklyn preachers asked black congregations not to drink beer in the grandstands. Mothers told their children to ignore racial comments. Soon signs appeared at the ballpark with Rickey's slogan: "Don't Spoil Jackie's Chances." There was never any trouble, and to show their appreciation the Brooklyn Dodgers held a Jackie Robinson Day near the end of the season before a packed stadium.

The Dodgers went on to win the National League pennant that fall as Robinson hit .297, finished first in the league in stolen bases, second in runs scored, and tied for the team lead in home runs with 12. As the National League champions, the Dodgers earned

Larry Doby, the first black to play in the American League, made his debut with the Cleveland Indians on July 5, 1947.

the right to meet their crosstown rivals from the American League, the New York Yankees, in the World Series.

"I guess if I could choose one of the most important moments in my life," Robinson said, "I would go back to 1947, in the Yankee Stadium in New York City. It was the opening day of the World Series and I was for the first time playing in the series as a member of the Brooklyn Dodgers team."

Although the Dodgers went on to lose the Series, four games to three, to a Yankee team that included Joe DiMaggio, Yogi Berra, and Phil Rizzuto, Robinson's presence there meant to him that he had finally made it. *The Sporting News*, baseball's leading newspaper, confirmed that "the great experiment" had indeed been a success. The paper, which had doubted his skills at the start of the season, named him Rookie of the Year. ✺

The Dodgers and their fans celebrate a win over the New York Yankees in a 1947 World Series game. Brooklyn's crosstown rivals eventually won the Series in seven games.

4

ON HIS
OWN

ROBINSON TOURED the South after his first major league season, speaking to black community groups and meeting many people. Often after a speech he enjoyed homecooked meals with black families who asked him to be their house guest. Partly as a result of their hospitality, he reported to the Dodgers' 1948 spring training camp 25 pounds overweight. This infuriated Leo Durocher, who had returned as manager after completing his one-year suspension. Durocher put Robinson on a rigorous workout schedule, but the conditioning program failed to help him. He started the year slowly; the brilliant aggressiveness that had characterized his first major league baseball season was noticeably absent. However, things started to click for him by mid-season, and a late-season hitting streak lifted Robinson's batting average to .296 for the year, which was good considering his slow start. He also hit 12 home runs and had 85 runs batted in. All told, his 1948 season reaffirmed that his rookie season had not been a fluke. But the Dodgers had a disappointing year and finished in third place.

One of the season's highlights occured when Roy Campanella became the second black to join the team. Another was when Robinson was thrown out of a game in Pittsburgh after a controversial call by the home plate umpire. Angered by the call,

Robinson usually ran into little trouble on the base paths, although he was caught here in a rundown by the Chicago Cubs in 1948. During his career, he led the National League twice in stolen bases.

53

Regarded by some as argumentative, Robinson maintained, "Many times when I made strong or controversial statements, I was not fighting for a personal thing. I was standing up for my team."

Dodger players heckled the umpire from the dugout. The umpire warned the team to stop, but the team, led by Robinson, persisted. The umpire finally tore off his mask and shouted to Robinson that he was being kicked out of the game.

Robinson was not singled out because he was black. He was treated like any other ballplayer who refused to listen to an umpire. "That made me feel great, even though I couldn't play any more that day," Robinson said. A newspaper headline said it best: "Jackie Just Another Guy."

Off the field, life for Robinson and his wife was far from ordinary. They were busy raising their son, Jackie Jr., who had been born in 1946, and had moved from New York City to Brooklyn, where they slowly found themselves being accepted by their predominantly white neighbors. The Robinsons became close friends with the Satlow family, whom they met in early 1948. Their children played together, and the parents often visited with each other in the evenings. The families never mentioned race or religion, a fact that became apparent on Christmas Eve in 1948.

As the Robinsons trimmed their holiday tree, the Satlow children watched with envy, having never seen a Christmas tree being decorated. Robinson believed it was because the family could not afford to buy one, so later that night he appeared at the family's front door carrying a large spruce. The Satlows were appreciative but soon made it clear to the Robinsons that they did not celebrate Christmas because they were Jewish. The Satlows recognized Robinson's good intentions and put up the tree anyway.

That winter proved to be a major turning point in Robinson's baseball career. As the first black to play major league baseball, he had always felt compelled to defend his rights and to speak his mind, but he had remained silent during his first two seasons, as Rickey had asked him to do. To remain silent had been difficult for a man who believed in swift retaliation and honest rebuttal. Remembering his childhood days, when a neighbor called him names, he felt, "I spoke my mind then. I should speak it now."

Rickey had observed Robinson's torment with a great deal of sympathy. "I could see how the tensions had built up in two years and that this young man had come through with courage far beyond what I asked," Rickey said. "I knew also that while the wisest policy for Robinson during those first two years was to turn the other cheek and not fight back, there were many in baseball who would not understand his lack of action. They could be made

Robinson with Rachel and three-month-old Jackie, Jr.

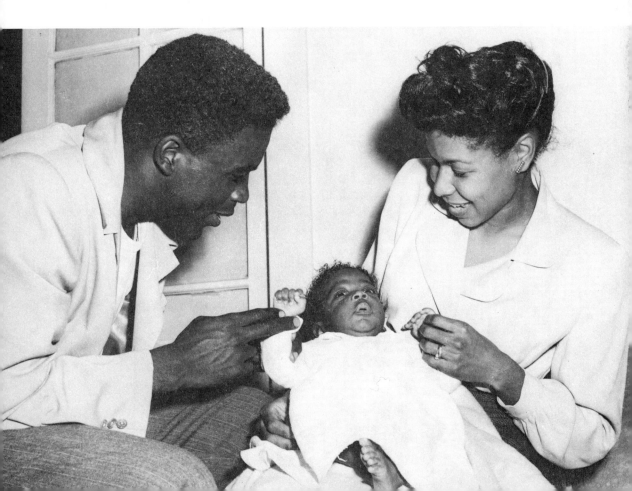

to respect only the fighting back, the things that are the signs of courage to men who know courage only in its physical sense."

Robinson had performed his pioneering role with courage and dignity. He had suffered silently so other black men, like Roy Campanella, could follow his path. With Campanella already on the club and Don Newcombe set to join it in 1949, Robinson no longer had to fight the battle by himself.

"Jackie, you're on your own now," Rickey told him that winter. "You can be yourself now."

Reporters caught their first glimpse of the new Jackie Robinson in spring training of 1949. During a routine interview, he issued a challenge to other big league ballplayers. "They'd better be rough on me this year, because I'm sure going to be rough on them," he told reporters. The remark brought a

Spring training, 1949. Robinson greets (from left to right) teammates Roy Campanella, Dan Bankhead, and Don Newcombe.

reprimand from major league officials, who believed the comment would cause racial trouble. It also marked the beginning of a long period of controversy in Robinson's baseball career.

While most players aired their views by talking with the press and saw their comments win respect and acclaim, Robinson was never afforded the same status. When he complained, people called him a crybaby or a complainer. Robinson once commented, "I learned that as long as I appeared to ignore insult and injury, I was a martyred hero to a lot of people who seemed to have sympathy for the underdog. But the minute I began to answer, to argue, to protest— the minute I began to sound off—I became a swellhead, a wise guy, an 'uppity' nigger. When a white guy did it, he had spirit. When a black player did it, he was 'ungrateful,' 'an upstart,' 'a sorehead.'"

Yet Robinson had been given the go-ahead to speak his mind, and he soon expressed his social and political beliefs to a nationwide audience. In July 1949 he testified before the House Un-American Activities Committee in Washington, D.C. He had been invited to speak before the committee in response to comments made by Paul Robeson, a famous black American actor and singer, who had told an audience in Paris that American blacks would not fight for America in a war against the Soviet Union. His comment had outraged American politicians, and they asked Robinson to address Robeson's statement.

Speaking before the committee, Robinson said, "I can't speak for fifteen million people any more than any other person can, but I know that I've got too much invested for my wife and child and myself in the future of this country, and I and other Americans of many races and faiths have too much invested in our country's welfare, for any of us to throw it away. . . . But that doesn't mean we're

Robinson and Rachel in Washington, D.C., for his testimony before the House Un-American Activities Committee in 1949.

going to stop fighting race discrimination in this country until we've got it licked. It means that we're going to fight it all the harder because our stake in the future is so big."

Robinson received tremendous praise for his affirmation of American ideals and immediately became a more popular player. His efforts on the baseball field in 1949 did little to hurt his growing popularity. The season was Robinson's best as a pro. He played with an intensity and skill that few players have ever shown. He finished the season with a .342 batting average—the highest in the league. He also led the league in stolen bases with 37 and placed among the league leaders in hits, runs scored, runs batted in, triples, and slugging percentage.

Defensively, Robinson was near perfect, sucking up ground balls at second base like a vacuum cleaner. He made the quick, stinging throws necessary for throwing out the baserunners. He turned more dou-

A familiar sight to baseball fans: Robinson completes another successful, daring steal of home, this time against the Boston Braves during the 1948 season.

Robinson surrounded by some of his trophies following the 1949 season, when he won the National League's Most Valuable Player Award.

ble plays than any second baseman in the National League, often converting seemingly impossible plays into routine outs.

By every measure, it was a magnificent year—one of the best ever recorded by a major leaguer. Sportswriters named him the league's Most Valuable Player. He soon signed a new contract with the Brooklyn Dodgers for $35,000—a huge amount in those days.

The only low point of the year occurred after the Dodgers had won the National League pennant. They again lost in the World Series to their cross-town rivals, the New York Yankees, this time in just five games.

5

THE
CONTROVERSIES
CONTINUE

ﾟﾟﾟﾟﾟﾟﾟﾟﾟﾟﾟﾟ

MOSTLY HAPPY TIMES continued for Robinson in 1950, as Rachel gave birth to their only daughter, Sharon. With the family requiring more living space, the Robinsons moved from Brooklyn to a racially mixed suburb in St. Albans, New York. Soon after this move Robinson embarked on a new challenge. Before the start of the 1950 baseball season, he starred in a film version of his life. *The Jackie Robinson Story* took only a few months to produce. Filmed in California, the movie told the story of how Robinson had become major league baseball's first black player.

Robinson enjoyed the experience, for acting in front of a camera was like performing before a crowd on a baseball diamond. He also appreciated the frills that came with acting in Hollywood. Each morning, a limousine greeted Robinson and his family at their hotel and transported them to the studio. The work provided a much-needed diversion from the pressures that came with playing baseball.

Critics panned the film when it premiered in May 1950, citing poor writing and direction, although they enjoyed Robinson's performance.

Mixed reviews could also be used to describe Robinson's family life at that time. Although he and Rachel were happy together, their children had some difficulties. Sharon and Jackie, Jr., would grow up

After Robinson's first few years with the Dodgers he noted that "there was a tremendous improvement in the closeness of the Dodger team. Racial tensions had almost completely dissipated."

living constantly in the shadow of their father. People pampered the children and made them feel different and uncomfortable. Jackie, Jr., was particularly affected by this kind of attention. He was always being compared to his talented, athletic father, with people often asking him if he was going to be as good a ballplayer as his dad.

Once a happy child, Jackie, Jr., would become moody and difficult as he grew older. He never learned to concentrate in school and received poor

Robinson teaches four-year-old Jackie, Jr., the proper batting stance during spring training in 1951.

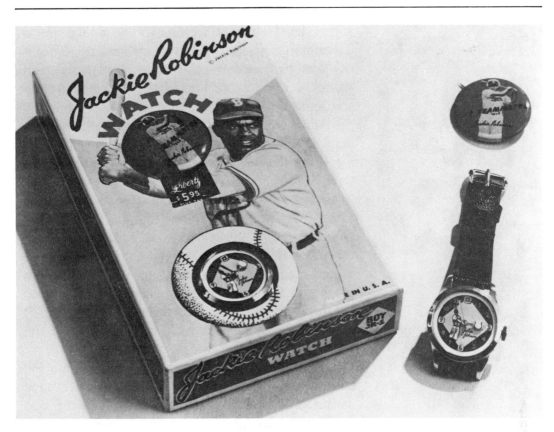

grades. He often refused to pose for photographs and would not listen to his parents. A deep division eventually formed between Jackie, Jr., and his father; the boy's bitterness and resentment grew ever stronger.

Back at the ballpark, life also had its difficulties. Although Robinson had become increasingly accepted, he still faced racial prejudice, as bigoted fans continued to object to black men playing major league baseball. They regarded Robinson as a contemptible symbol of black progress in American society. Some bigots even made death threats against Robinson and his family.

The most serious incident occurred during the 1950 season. The Dodgers received a letter in which the writer threatened to kill Robinson if he played

Robinson's popularity with the Dodgers' fans led to the creation of such promotional items as a Jackie Robinson watch.

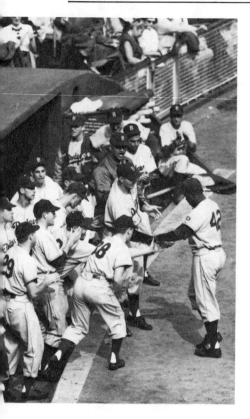

Robinson is greeted by his teammates after his two-run homer gave the Dodgers the lead in the second game of their 1951 three-game playoff series against the New York Giants.

at Crosley Field in Cincinnati. The police and a Cincinnati newspaper received similar letters. Security was tightened for the game. Undercover FBI agents and police officers patrolled the grandstands and searched nearby buildings for possible snipers.

Before the game, Robinson was tense but confident nothing would happen. Teammates tried to break the tension by joking that all of them should wear Robinson's number to confuse the gunman.

Despite the pressure on him, Robinson won the game with a late-inning home run. Cal Abrams, the Dodgers' Jewish outfielder, who had also received threats during the season, scored on the hit. Abrams waited for Robinson to cross home plate and then escorted him quickly to the dugout. "Let's not stand out here in full view of everyone," he urged. "If they are ever gonna shoot the two of us, now's the time."

The 1950 season went on without incident and ended on an upbeat note for Robinson. He finished with a .328 batting average and recorded the best fielding percentage of any second baseman in the National League. The Dodgers, however, lost their chance to win the league championship on the last day of the season, beaten out just barely by Philadelphia. It was the first of what would be many heartbreaking losses for Robinson and the Dodgers over the next few years.

One of the losses occurred off the field, when Branch Rickey resigned as president of the Brooklyn Dodgers. After a bitter power struggle with Rickey, Walter O'Malley, a strong-willed Dodger executive, took control of the team. O'Malley resented Robinson because he had a close friendship with the Dodgers' former boss. Robinson caused further trouble by announcing his continued loyalty to Rickey. Over the years O'Malley and Robinson's relationship grew openly hostile.

However, the two men's mutual dislike for each other did not affect the team's 1951 performance. Brooklyn battled their archrivals, the New York Giants, the entire season for first place. The Giants clinched a tie for the championship by defeating the Boston Braves on the last day of the season. Later that same day the Dodgers faced the Philadelphia Phillies. The Dodgers needed a win to be in a three-game playoff with the Giants.

This all-important game proved to be a showcase for Robinson as he put on one of his finest performances. The Phillies jumped out to an early lead, and by the fourth inning led 6–1. The Dodgers managed to tie the score at 8 with a three-run rally in the eighth, and the crucial game went into extra innings. With two outs and the potential winning run on third base in the twelfth inning, a Phillies

Robinson slides in safely on the front end of a double steal.

batter slapped a looping fly ball over second base. It looked like a sure hit to drive in what would be the winning run, but Robinson, playing second base, raced to his right and dove through the air, spearing the sinking ball. He hit the ground hard and stayed there for a moment. No one knew whether he had held onto the ball. Finally, Robinson staggered to his feet and proudly raised his glove with the ball still in it.

Having narrowly escaped defeat, the Dodgers continued the game with Robinson playing half dazed by the fall he had taken. In the top of the 14th inning, he again came to bat. Sensing Robinson's weariness, Robin Roberts, an eventual Hall of Fame pitcher, threw what he thought would be an over-powering fastball. Robinson's swing sent the ball deep into the left-field bleachers for a home run that gave the Dodgers the win, 9–8. It also sent the team into a three-game playoff series with the New York Giants for the National League crown.

As a second baseman Robinson led the National League in fielding percentage three times—including 1951, when he set an all-time mark for the position.

The series was to live in baseball lore as a classic. The teams split for the first two games. In the third game, Robinson again played well in what was to become one of the most famous games ever played. He scored the team's first run, and by the bottom of the ninth inning the Dodgers were still leading, 4–2, with victory close at hand. But with two outs and runners at second and third, the Giants' Bobby Thomson unloaded a three-run home run off Dodger pitcher Ralph Branca. Now known as "The Shot Heard Around the World," the hit won the game for the Giants and killed the Dodgers' hopes of playing in the World Series.

This defeat was typical of the Brooklyn Dodgers. The team often came close to winning a world championship, only to come up short late in the season. Fans familiar with the team's problems would cry, "Wait till next year." To be a Brooklyn Dodgers fan meant being both pessimistic and optimistic.

The jinx continued through 1952, as the Dodgers won the National League pennant in late September but lost to the New York Yankees in the World Series, four games to three.

Robinson did not play well in the series, recording only four hits in 23 trips to home plate. But even worse was the bitter humiliation he had suffered during the season. Throughout 1952 a controversy raged in the sports pages of America's leading newspapers. The papers compared the outspoken Jackie Robinson with his black teammate Roy Campanella, who shunned attention. Campanella often disagreed with Robinson's views on baseball and politics but kept silent about how he felt. The press praised Campanella for his reserve and often wondered why Robinson, who took advantage of almost every available opportunity to protest racial discrimination, could not act similarly.

Yankee Stadium is also known as "The House That Ruth Built" because the ballpark was originally erected to hold the huge crowds that wanted to see the legendary Babe Ruth play with the Yankees in the 1920s and 1930s.

Dick Young, a sportswriter with the New York *Daily News*, explained the situation to Robinson. "The trouble between you and me, Jackie," Young said, "is that I can go to Campy and all we discuss is baseball. I talk to you and sooner or later we get around to social issues . . . a lot of newspapermen are saying that Campy's the kind of guy they can like but that your aggressiveness, your wearing your race on your sleeve, makes enemies."

Robinson told Young that he was proud of what he was: a responsible black who was tired of being patient. "If it makes some people uncomfortable, if it makes me the kind of guy they can't like, that's tough."

Robinson's response was typical of his approach to such controversy. In November 1953 he was

Robinson and Roy Campanella after their first season together with the Dodgers, instructing young members of the Harlem YMCA.

invited to be on "Youth Wants to Know," a television show that had him answering questions asked by a young studio audience. When a teenage girl from the audience asked him, "Mr. Robinson, do you think the Yankees are prejudiced against Negro players?" he answered with characteristic honesty. Robinson said, " I think the Yankee management is prejudiced. There isn't a single Negro on the team now and very few in the entire Yankee farm system."

Robinson's candid response caused many people to think that he was trying to stir up trouble—that he had intentionally used the television show to air views. A great controversy arose as newspaper columns and letters to the Dodgers' front office attacked Robinson's motives. Robinson's uneasiness about the entire affair was put to rest after Ford

Robinson and Roy Campanella (at left) may have differed in their opinions on how to handle black issues, but, according to Robinson, they never had a personal quarrel.

The first black players to be invited to an All-Star Game. Appearing in the 1949 contest were (from left to right) Roy Campanella, Larry Doby, Don Newcombe, and Jackie Robinson.

Frick, who had been made baseball commissioner in 1951, asked to speak with him in person. Robinson was told that he would be supported by the commissioner whenever Robinson felt the need to speak out strongly on a racial issue.

Robinson's views were heard most often by the sportswriters who covered the team on a daily basis. Some criticized his forthrightness, while others understood and sympathized with him. But no matter whether people sided with him or were against him, Robinson carried on, becoming one of the most outspoken athletes of his generation. Young seemed to sum up both the pros and cons of Robinson's actions when the New York sportswriter wrote in one of his columns about Robinson: "He has the tact of a child because he has the moral purity of a child."

Controversy followed Robinson away from the field as well. After the birth of his second son, David, in 1952, the Robinsons began looking for a new, larger home. The search proved long and difficult, since many New York suburbs were closed to black families in the early 1950s because of discrimination. Each time the Robinsons discovered a house they liked, the owner or real-estate agent gave a reason why the family could not buy it. After the family found a house in Purchase, New York, the owner mysteriously pulled it off the market. In other

During his years with the Dodgers, Robinson consistently led the team in runs scored.

Stan Musial of the St. Louis Cardinals congratulates Robinson in 1952 after the Dodger second baseman hit his first home run in an All-Star game.

instances, sellers inflated their prices after they learned that the Robinsons were black.

Finally, after two years, a newspaper ran a story on the Robinsons' plight. Community leaders were outraged by the treatment shown to the family and worked to find the Robinsons a home. In 1955 the family moved to a house in Stamford, Connecticut. The Robinsons were the only black family in Stamford, and Jackie, Jr., Sharon, and David all felt uncomfortable as the only black children in an all-white neighborhood. Robinson thought this situation was simply a fact of life:

> I am not a fanatical integrationist. I don't think there is any particular magic in a white kid sitting next to a black kid in a classroom. . . . I also believe both black and white children can gain something by being able to relate to each other.
>
> I am opposed to enforced separatism and I am opposed to enforced segregation. The first freedom for all people is freedom of choice. . . . I want to be free to follow the dictates of my own mind and conscience without being subject to the pressures of any man, black or white. I think that is what most people of all races want. Unfortunately, it is not what black people in this country have. Until we do we will continue to live in a farcical society, and the high principles on which America was founded will continue to be distorted. ☙

6

MIXED BLESSINGS

I N THE YEARS following Robinson's arrival on the scene, desegregation in baseball did not proceed very rapidly. By the end of the 1953 season, only 6 of the 16 major league teams had black ballplayers on their rosters. Many of the owners maintained that there were not enough black ballplayers who were ready to play in the major leagues—the Negro Leagues had most of the best black players. Yet blacks had won the Rookie of the Year Award in every year except one following Robinson's debut in 1947, and they had also won the Most Valuable Player Award three times. The owners, it seemed, were signing only black ballplayers who would be stars.

Robinson continued to be one of those stars during the 1953 season. He batted .329 and scored 109 runs as the Brooklyn Dodgers compiled an impressive record of 105 wins and 49 losses and again won the National League pennant. At season's end they faced the New York Yankees once more in the World Series. Once again the Yankees won, again in seven games, despite a .320 batting performance by Robinson.

The following winter the Dodgers signed Walter

Manager Walter Alston (right) stands by Walter O'Malley, who became the principal owner and president of the Dodgers in 1950 after defeating Branch Rickey in a struggle for control of the club.

Ebbets Field in Brooklyn, New York, was the home of the Dodgers until the end of the 1957 season, after which the team moved west to Los Angeles.

Alston to manage the team with the hope that he could bring them a world championship. Unlike the other Dodger managers for whom Robinson had played—Burt Shotton, Leo Durocher, and Charlie Dressen—Alston was strict and unfriendly. He rarely showed emotion or talked with his players. Robinson did not like Alston's style, which he considered too conservative for the Brooklyn Dodgers.

An incident in Chicago during the 1954 season dramatized their differences. Duke Snider of the Dodgers hit a fly ball to deep center field. After seeing the ball bounce back onto the playing field, the second-base umpire claimed that the ball had hit the center-field wall and ruled it simply a base

A huge crowd at Ebbets Field watches the 1953 World Series matchup between the Dodgers and the New York Yankees.

hit. Robinson saw the play differently. He believed that the ball had struck a spectator and under the rules should count as a home run. To state his case, Robinson left the dugout and argued nose to nose with the umpire.

During the exchange, Alston never moved or said a word. He remained in the third-base coaching box with his hands on his hips. Robinson later blasted Alston for his indifference, saying, "If that guy hadn't stood standing there at third base like a wooden Indian, this club might be going somewhere. Here's a play that meant a run in a tight ball game, so whether I was right or wrong, the play was close enough to protest to the umpire."

A photograph printed in the next day's newspaper clearly showed that Robinson had been correct: a fan had touched the ball. Alston, however, seemed unwilling to forgive Robinson for the "wooden Indian" remark and played him less frequently after his outburst.

The incident marked the beginning of the end of Robinson's playing career. At 35 years old, his body had started to slow down. He recorded fewer hits and stole fewer bases. Much of his brilliant speed was gone. To hide his slowing reflexes, the Dodgers moved him from second base to the outfield. But the move did not help the team enough and the Dodgers finished the 1954 season in second place.

In baseball, hope springs eternal, as each new season offers a fresh start. For Robinson, 1955 marked

Yankee Stadium in the Bronx, New York, was the site of many exciting World Series meetings between the Dodgers and the Yankees.

his last great hurrah. It was an especially sweet moment to have as he neared retirement.

The Dodgers played spectacular baseball that year. The pitching staff was the class of the league. Some new young players helped the hitters pace the league in batting average and home runs. The Dodgers finished 13½ games in front of the second-place finishers.

Robinson did not play as much during the season as he had in the past, and he ended the year with a mediocre .256 batting average—the lowest of his career. Newpaper reporters speculated that he would soon retire. However, he played like a spirited youngster in the 1955 World Series. In what had seemingly become an autumn tradition, the Series pitted the Dodgers against the New York Yankees.

The Dodgers fell behind quickly in the first game of the Series. By the top of the eighth inning they trailed the Yankees, 6–4, with Robinson at third base and two outs. He watched the first pitch pass for a ball and noticed that neither the pitcher nor the catcher paid him much attention. So, on the next pitch, Robinson suddenly broke down the third base line and barreled toward the plate. He arrived there at the same time as the ball, but his slide caused the catcher to miss the tag. He had stolen home.

Even though the Dodgers lost the first game, Robinson's aggressive play sparked the team. They played courageously throughout the Series, with Robinson's gutsy baserunning and defense helping them to split the first six games with the Yankees. In the Series finale, the Brooklyn Dodgers won, 2–0, and earned their first and only world championship. "It was one of the greatest thrills of my life to be finally on a World Series winner," Robinson said after the victory.

Don Larsen of the Yankees on his way to becoming the only pitcher in baseball history to throw a perfect game in the World Series. He did it by whitewashing the Dodgers in the 1956 classic.

*Win or lose, loyal Brooklyn
Dodger fans always rooted enthu-
siastically for their team.*

The following year marked Robinson's last season of major league baseball. At age 37, he was a
mere shadow of his younger self, even though he
played in over two-thirds of the Dodgers' games and
finished the year with a .275 batting average. His
not-so-great performance in the 1956 World Series,
which the Dodgers lost to the Yankees, four games
to three, brought his lifetime World Series batting
average to .234.

Throughout the 1956 season, Robinson quietly
planned his retirement. On several occasions he met
with William Black, president of Chock Full O'Nuts,
a large restaurant chain based in New York City.
Black wanted Robinson to join the company as
vice-president of community affairs.

It was an intriguing offer since Robinson had always been interested in business. As his sister, Willa Mae, stated, "From the moment Jackie came to the major leagues, he never stopped looking for other employment opportunities. He never knew if he was going to make it at first and how long he was going to last." But before Robinson accepted the job offer, the Dodgers made several landmark announcements. One was that Ebbets Field, the team's home park, was to be sold. The Dodgers were moving to Los Angeles.

The decision bitterly upset Dodgers fans. They had supported the Brooklyn franchise in the National League for over 65 years. Now, two years after they had won their first World Series, the Dodger management would be moving the team to the warmer weather and bigger crowds of Southern California.

Choosing to retire in 1957 rather than play for the New York Giants, Robinson turned down his chance to play alongside home run king Willie Mays (crossing plate).

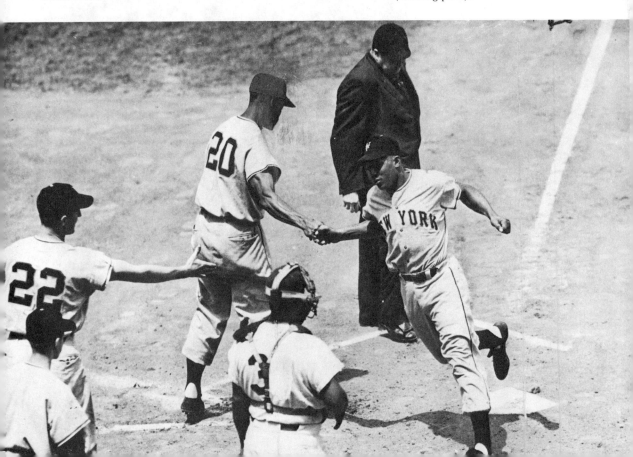

The Dodgers also announced that, in preparation for relocation, Robinson was being traded to the New York Giants for $35,000. The move shocked Robinson. Even though he knew trades were part of the game, he felt rejected when the news broke. At the same time, he was flattered by the Giants' interest. The team believed Robinson had a few good years left. It also wanted him to play alongside Willie Mays, the Giants' brilliant young center fielder. The team believed the Mays-Robinson combination would lure many fans to the ballpark. As an enticement to Robinson, the Giants offered him a $60,000 salary, which was a huge amount of money in 1956.

But Robinson was a man of principles. "It would be unfair to the Giants and their fans to take their

The Robinson family in their Stamford, Connecticut, home in 1957. Along with Jackie and Rachel are (from right to left) Sharon, Jackie, Jr., and David.

money," he said. "The Giants are a team that need youth and rebuilding. The team doesn't need me."

Robinson never played in a New York Giant uniform. In January 1957 he retired from baseball. To his family, Robinson's retirement meant an end to long road trips and late night games, but it also marked the start of some new challenges. 🐾

Robinson packing up his baseball gear in January 1957 after announcing his retirement from the game.

7

A PASSION
FOR
POLITICS

MANY FAMOUS ATHLETES who retire from
professional sports accept positions with major com-
panies as figureheads. They appear at special events
and lend their names to company projects, gaining
valuable public exposure for the company but performing little of the real work. They become celeb-
rity spokespeople who have little to say in the
company they represent.

Robinson refused such an arrangement after his
retirement from the Brooklyn Dodgers. Before joining Chock Full O'Nuts as vice-president of community relations, he made one point absolutely clear:
he wanted to be an important part of the company.
He demanded an active role in management and
administration.

The company agreed, and Robinson worked to
strengthen the company's name and reputation in
the community. He was especially sensitive to the
needs of black employees who worked as cooks and
waitresses for the company.

The transition to business came easily to Robinson as he quickly adapted his competitive nature to
the business world. His work helped him gain valuable insight into money, power, and politics. He

*Robinson meets with Richard Nixon, the Republican candidate
in the 1960 presidential election.*

85

The headline tells the story: the Supreme Court ruled in May 1954 that segregation in public schools was unconstitutional.

realized that blacks could use these tools to improve their place in American society. He later said, "During the post-baseball years, I became increasingly persuaded that there were two keys to the advancement of blacks in America—the ballot and the buck."

Robinson believed that blacks could gain more influence by organizing their economic and political efforts. This belief gave new importance to his life. In the following years he became an important figure in politics, business, and the civil rights movement as he worked to advance the rights of black people.

Robinson's first taste of politics occurred in the late 1950s. While working for Chock Full O'Nuts, he was asked to head a fund-raising campaign for the National Association for the Advancement of Colored People (NAACP), an influential civil rights group. Chock Full O'Nuts allowed him to travel and speak for the organization, as long as his efforts did not interfere with company work.

As a spokesman for the NAACP Robinson spoke to black community groups, urging them to support equal rights for all Americans and asking for their financial help in supporting the NAACP. The work exhilarated him. "I started out talking for five or ten minutes at these meetings, and when I got going, well, I was doing half-hour speeches," Robinson said. "It was a thrill to learn that it is not true that black people are not willing to pay for their free-

Robinson in 1960, picketing a store in Cleveland whose branches in the South refused to serve blacks. The protest was supported by the National Association for the Advancement of Colored People (NAACP).

The 1954 Supreme Court ruling against segregation failed to ease racial tensions completely. In September 1957 federal troops were needed to guard black students on their way to classes in Little Rock, Arkansas.

dom." An eloquent speaker, he proved to be a successful fund-raiser for the NAACP.

Robinson's civil rights work placed him in a difficult situation during the 1960 presidential election, which pitted Richard M. Nixon against John F. Kennedy. Both politicians wanted Robinson to work for their campaigns since they believed his support would win over black voters.

Robinson decided to meet the candidates before making a decision to work for one of them. He first met with Nixon, the Republican candidate, who was then vice-president under President Dwight D. Eisenhower. The meeting left Robinson impressed. Next, he met with Senator Kennedy, a Massachusetts Democrat. The meeting went poorly. Although

John F. Kennedy on the campaign trail during the 1960 presidential race.

Robinson with Dr. Martin Luther King, Jr., in 1962. "I was immediately struck by his dedication," Robinson said. "I joined him whenever possible."

Kennedy impressed Robinson with his knowledge of foreign affairs, farm problems, urban crises, and so on, he appeared to be uneducated on civil rights. "This was a man who had served in the Senate and wanted to be President but who knew little or nothing about black problems and sensibilities," Robinson said. "He himself admitted a lack of any depth of understanding about black people."

Robinson supported Nixon in the 1960 election, campaigning heavily for his victory, but Kennedy won the election and a sizable majority of the black vote. Kennedy, as it turned out, worked hard for black civil rights once he became president. He supported Dr. Martin Luther King, Jr., the great civil rights leader, and sent armed troops into Southern schools to enforce desegregation of education.

Many black voters never forgave Robinson for supporting Nixon. Years later, Robinson admitted making an error, saying, "I do not consider my decision to back Richard Nixon over John F. Kennedy for the Presidency in 1960 one of my finer ones. It was a sincere one, however, at the time."

Besides politics, baseball was again on Robinson's mind in 1962 as he became eligible for induction into the Baseball Hall of Fame in Cooperstown, New York. Induction is the highest honor a profes-

Robinson worked hard for the improvement of black civil rights. He is shown here picketing a construction site in Brooklyn in 1963.

Dr. Martin Luther King, Jr., (front line, fourth from right) leads a group of protesters in a march against segregation. This protest took place in Washington, D.C., in August 1963.

Robinson and heavyweight champion Floyd Patterson about to board a plane in May 1963 to fly to a civil rights demonstration in Birmingham, Alabama.

sional ballplayer can receive. To qualify a player must have been retired from the game for at least five years and have made a significant contribution to the game of baseball.

Robinson's contributions certainly qualified as significant. As a ballplayer he compiled a lifetime batting average of .311 in a game in which anything over .300 is considered outstanding, and he averaged almost 100 runs scored each year. He won Rookie of the Year honors in 1947 and the Most Valuable Player Award in 1949. He led the league in stolen bases in 1947 and 1949; in fielding percentage in 1948, 1950, and 1951, and played in six

World Series. As the first black major league ball-player, he opened the sport to many other young black men.

Election to the Hall of Fame is determined by a vote of the Baseball Writers of America. Many sports-writers who were voting seemed to dislike Robinson because of his brutal honesty, so he did not believe he would be inducted in 1962. "Since I was a controversial personality in the eyes of the press, I steeled myself for rejection," he said.

Robinson flanked by his wife, Rachel, and Branch Rickey upon being inducted into baseball's Hall of Fame in 1962.

However, on January 23, 1962, Robinson received a telephone call at his home in Stamford, Connecticut, informing him that 124 of the 160

ROBINSON'S MAJOR LEAGUE STATISTICS

———— ❧ ————

BROOKLYN DODGERS
National League

Year	G	AB	R	H	2B	3B	HR	RBI	SB	AVG
1947	151	590	125	175	31	5	12	48	29	.297
1948	147	574	108	170	38	8	12	85	32	.296
1949	156	593	122	203	38	12	16	124	37	.342
1950	144	518	99	170	39	4	14	81	12	.328
1951	153	548	106	185	33	7	19	88	25	.338
1952	149	510	104	157	17	3	19	75	24	.308
1953	136	484	109	159	34	7	12	95	17	.329
1954	124	386	62	120	22	4	15	59	7	.311
1955	105	317	51	81	6	2	8	36	12	.256
1956	117	357	61	98	15	2	10	43	12	.275
Totals	1382	4877	947	1518	273	54	137	734	197	.311

William Black, the president of Chock Full O'Nuts. After hiring the former Dodger, Black allowed Robinson to work for the NAACP on company time.

ballots cast were in favor of his induction. Later in the year, he stood on a podium in Cooperstown, New York, in front of his peers and thanked the fans and his teammates for their support and Branch Rickey for his courage and conviction. With that, he became an official Hall of Famer. One of the game's great warriors, he felt at peace with major league baseball.

Back home in Stamford after the ceremony, life slowly returned to normal. Robinson continued to work at Chock Full O'Nuts. In the evenings and on weekends he pursued his political and social interests. With the children in school, Rachel furthered her education. She earned a master's degree in nursing from New York University. Later, she taught at Yale University School of Nursing. The younger children, David and Sharon, also did well in school. However, Jackie, Jr., presented serious problems. He often failed to complete assignments and turn in papers. He sometimes stayed out late without telling his parents. He rarely talked to his father.

Once, Jackie, Jr., ran away from home, hitchhiking across the country to California. Unable to find work, he finally telephoned his parents for money and returned home.

Father and son became painfully aware of their widening differences yet remained unable to get through to one another. Robinson said, "I loved him deeply and he knew it. But the peculiar chemistry that is responsible for free communication between two individuals was absent."

In the spring of 1964 Jackie, Jr., volunteered for the army. He thought the discipline of the army would help him sort out his life. His parents were less sure, especially since the United States was fighting in Vietnam at the time. Within the year, Jackie, Jr., was in combat.

The fall of 1964 brought another presidential election. Robinson, whose interest in politics was still strong, was particularly taken with Nelson Rockefeller, the governor of New York and a Republican candidate for the presidential nomination. The two men had first met in 1962 after Robinson wrote a letter to Rockefeller attacking the governor for failing to provide jobs for blacks in New York state government. In a meeting that followed, Robinson outlined steps the governor should take to hire more blacks.

Rockefeller's quick response to some of Robinson's employment suggestions left Robinson impressed. In the past, politicians often listened politely to Robinson's objections, but rarely did they act. So, when Rockefeller asked for his support, Robinson was happy to oblige. "I wanted to involve myself in

Following his move from the dugout to a desk, Robinson said, "I was even with baseball and baseball with me. The game had done much for me, and I had done much for it."

Robinson aided Governor Nelson Rockefeller in the politician's bid to become the Republican nominee for president in 1964.

politics as a means of helping black people," he said, and thought that this was the perfect opportunity. After some deliberation, Robinson resigned from Chock Full O'Nuts and joined Rockefeller's campaign as a special assistant to the governor.

Robinson campaigned hard for Rockefeller, even though he was in an odd position for a black man. Blacks usually supported candidates of the more liberal Democratic party. But Robinson defended his Republican position, contending that it was important that the Republican party not turn completely white. He met with white and black community groups all over the nation, at each stop explaining the governor's views on political issues.

Robinson performed tirelessly, but his labor was to no avail. Rockefeller lost the Republican nomination for president to Barry Goldwater, a conservative senator from Arizona, who later lost the presidential election to Lyndon B. Johnson, a Democrat from Texas.

Robinson considered the loss a serious setback to race relations in the United States. "I admit freely that I think, live, and breathe black first and foremost," he said. "That is one of the reasons I was so committed to the governor and so opposed to Senator Barry Goldwater."

Robinson left the campaign bitter and disenchanted, but defeat in one area led to victory in another. After the 1964 election he helped to establish the Freedom National Bank. The bank was a black-owned and -operated financial institution located in Harlem in New York City. Robinson and other black businessmen started the bank to loan money to black businessmen, a service that was desperately needed since white-owned banks rarely financed black businesses, believing that blacks were bad credit risks.

Robinson helped raise more than $1.5 million to start the bank. He then served on its board of directors, which oversaw the bank's operation. The Freedom National Bank, which became a source of pride in Harlem, financed many new businesses and provided money for community projects. ◆

8

TRAGEDY
AND
TRIUMPH

❧

THE SECOND HALF of the 1960s was a difficult and sorrowful time for Robinson. In December 1965 Branch Rickey died. The relationship between Rickey and Robinson has often been likened to that of a father and a son. "There was an alliance between them and a kind of mutual respect," said Rachel Robinson. The loss of Rickey affected Robinson deeply.

Robinson's grief mounted in 1968 when his mother passed away while tending her garden in Pasadena.

There were other family tragedies as well. In 1967 Jackie, Jr., was wounded in action in Vietnam. He returned home more confused than before he had left. One of the things he did was to smoke marijuana and tell his parents that the drug was not addictive. The Robinsons tried to believe him. "We knew things weren't right, but there is nothing that can blind parents as much as loving hope," Robinson said. "We found out later that there is something about drug addiction that imbues its victims with a terrible sense of craftiness and ingenuity. Jack sold us on his point of view."

The full scope of Jackie, Jr.'s, drug addiction surfaced in 1968 when he was arrested on charges of possession and carrying a concealed weapon. Shocked and angered by the news, Robinson felt like disown-

"I had to deny my true fighting spirit so that the 'noble experiment' could succeed," Robinson said. "But I never cared about acceptance as much as I cared about respect."

Robinson and Rachel at a pregame ceremony during the 1972 World Series commemorating the 25th anniversary of his entrance into baseball.

ing his son. But he also wanted to offer support, so he went to the police station and posted bail. After a long talk, the Robinsons discovered that Jackie, Jr.'s, problems were much greater than they had imagined.

After entering the army, Jackie, Jr., fought his boredom with basic training by drinking beer and smoking marijuana. When he transferred to Vietnam, his drug use increased as he soon began to experiment with other drugs. To block out the harsh realities of war, he turned to cocaine and heroin, until he had developed a drug habit that he could not break. He started stealing once he was home from the war so he would have money to buy drugs. This led to his carrying handguns and knives, for which he was arrested.

"When the roof caved in," said Robinson, "when Jackie got into deep trouble, I realized that I had been so busy trying to help other youngsters that I had neglected my own." After hearing their son's story, the Robinsons decided to support him fully.

The court offered Jackie, Jr., two alternatives: either he go to prison, or he could admit himself to a drug rehabilitation program. He chose rehabilitation and entered a program in Connecticut where the program's counselors were reformed addicts. They told Jackie and Rachel Robinson that their son had a long road in front of him. Physical addiction required only days to break. Mental addiction took much longer.

Fortunately for all concerned, Jackie, Jr., had the inner strength to fight drug addiction. After one year in rehabilitation he was released from the program and soon began working there as a counselor. Jackie, Jr., dedicated the rest of his life to helping other addicts. Over the next few years he assisted many youths in overcoming their drug dependence.

Unfortunately, Jackie, Jr.'s, story did not end happily. On June 17, 1971, he was killed when his car skidded out of control and hit an embankment. Police broke the news early that morning to his father, who nearly collapsed. He later said, "You just don't lose a boy after finding him again and not really feel it." Yet many of the addicts whom Jackie, Jr., had counseled attended his funeral, and seeing all the people whom Jackie, Jr., had helped provided some solace to his father. "A life is not important except in the impact it has on others," Robinson often told young people, ultimately realizing that his son had led a very important life.

Robinson saw his own life begin to deteriorate as well in the early 1970s as his body became ravaged by the effects of diabetes and heart disease. In June 1972 he made one of his last public appearances, attending a ceremony at Dodger Stadium in Los Angeles to commemorate the 25th anniversary of

Robinson's funeral on October 27, 1972. The pallbearers included basketball great Bill Russell and former Dodger teammates Ralph Branca and Don Newcombe. Roy Campanella watches from his wheelchair.

his first major league season. As he stepped onto the field, the crowd could detect little resemblance to the brash young man who had once worn number 42 for the Dodgers. His hair had turned white, he walked with a limp due to a leg ailment, and he had lost nearly all of his eyesight. Yet he still managed to walk across the baseball diamond to watch the Dodgers retire his number.

Robinson died from a heart attack just a few months later, on October 24, 1972, leaving behind a legacy of great accomplishments. As an athlete, he electrified millions with his power and speed; his whirlwind style of base running and his natural hit-

ting ability are still revered today by the game's
followers. As the first black to play major league
baseball, he became a pioneer for black athletes in
professional sports. He faced scorn and prejudice
with courage and conviction. He believed deeply in
the expanding role of blacks in American sports and
society and fought tirelessly to see his dream become
a reality. And he did it on his own terms.

Robinson maintained throughout his life that
"the most luxurious possession, the richest treasure
anybody has, is his personal dignity." By succeeding
in baseball's great experiment, Jackie Robinson ena-
bled his rewards to be shared by many. ☙

CHRONOLOGY

January 31, 1919	Born Jack Roosevelt Robinson in Cairo, Georgia
May 1920	Robinson family moves to Pasadena, California
September 1933	Robinson enrolls at John Muir Technical High School
September 1937	Enrolls at Pasadena Junior College
September 1939	Enrolls at UCLA
1942–44	Serves in the Army
1945	Plays Negro League baseball for the Kansas City Monarchs
August 28, 1945	First meeting with Branch Rickey; signs contract to play for the Montreal Royals in the Brooklyn Dodgers' organization
April 18, 1946	Plays first game for the Montreal Royals
1946	Marries Rachel Isum; Royals win the Little World Series championship
November 1946	Jackie Robinson, Jr., is born
April 15, 1947	Robinson plays first game for the Brooklyn Dodgers
1947	Named National League Rookie of the Year; leads National League in stolen bases
July 1949	Testifies before the House Un-American Activities Committee
1949	Wins National League Most Valuable Player Award; leads National League in batting average and stolen bases
January 1950	Sharon Robinson is born
1950	Stars in film biography, *The Jackie Robinson Story*; Robinson family moves to St. Albans, New York; Branch Rickey resigns as president of the Dodgers
May 1952	David Robinson is born
1955	Robinson family moves to Stamford, Connecticut; Brooklyn Dodgers win the World Series
1956	Ebbets Field sold; Dodgers announce move to Los Angeles; Robinson traded to the New York Giants
January 1957	Announces retirement from baseball
1957	Joins Chock Full O'Nuts as vice-president for community relations; chairs NAACP fund drive
1960	Campaigns for Richard M. Nixon
January 23, 1962	Elected into the Baseball Hall of Fame
1964	Campaigns for Nelson Rockefeller; helps establish the Freedom National Bank
1968	Robinson's mother, Mallie, dies
June 1971	Robinson's son Jackie, Jr., killed in automobile accident
October 24, 1972	Robinson dies in Stamford, Connecticut

FURTHER READING

Frommer, Harvey. *Jackie Robinson*. New York: Franklin Watts, 1984.

Goldstein, Richard. *Spartan Seasons*. New York: Macmillan, 1980.

Kahn, Roger. *The Boys of Summer*. New York: Harper & Row, 1972.

Peterson, Robert. *Only the Ball Was White*. New York: McGraw-Hill, 1984.

Ritter, Lawrence S. *The Glory of Their Times*. New York: Morrow, 1984.

Robinson, Jackie. *I Never Had It Made*. New York: G. P. Putnam's Sons, 1972.

Rogosin, Donn. *Invisible Men*. New York: Atheneum, 1985.

Tygiel, Jules. *Baseball's Great Experiment*. New York: Oxford University Press, 1983.

Voigt, David Quentin. *American Baseball*. 3 volumes. University Park and London: Pennsylvania State University Press, 1983.

INDEX

Page numbers in italics refer to illustrations.

PICTURE CREDITS

————— ❧ —————

RICHARD SCOTT is a senior editor at a major publishing house in New York City. He is a graduate of Haverford College, where he studied literature and creative writing. His publishing career has given him the opportunity to work on books about subjects that he enjoys, including sports. He has been a participant in several marathons, although he is not as fast or as daring a runner as Jackie Robinson was.